OVERCOME THE
SPELLING
BLOCK

THE HOME HELP FOR NON-SPELLERS

GW00640770

OVERCOME THE
SPELLING
BLOCK

THE HOME HELP FOR NON-SPELLERS

Joyce Hallmark and
Molly Withers

foulsham

LONDON•NEW YORK•TORONTO•SYDNEY

foulsham

Yeovil Road, Slough, Berkshire SL1 4JH

ISBN 0-572-01690-5

Copyright © W. Foulsham & Co. Ltd 1992

Printed in Great Britain at the Maple Press, Slough.

The lyf so short, the craft so long to lerne,
Th' assay so hard, so sharp the conquerynge.

Geoffrey Chaucer 1340-1400 –
in the original fourteenth century spelling.

This guide is dedicated to Stephen,
whose cheerful tenacity is an example to us all.

TABLE OF CONTENTS

CHAPTER 1

UNDERSTANDING & HELPING NON-SPELLERS

Parents and helpers may sadly be all too familiar with "code" words like the following: "picre" (prince); "heaged" (hedge); "con . . ." (conclusion -. . . unable to finish the word); "wireting" (writing); "stirburrys" (strawberries); "frist" (first) and "inforshun" (information). The ten and eleven year olds, from many different schools, who wrote these and other "code" words could all read. However, sufficient resources were not available for these children to receive adequate extra help with their spelling problems during their primary school years.

This guide, the fruits of the many years' experience of a Clinical Psychologist and an English teacher turned specialist spelling tutor, offers explanations, detailed methods which have proved successful in practice and, most important, HOPE to concerned parents, husbands or wives, who wish to help their "students".

The guide includes:
1. a thorough grounding in the basics
2. handy hints and memory aids
3. more advanced spelling rules and their exceptions
4. advice on correcting errors constructively
5. advice on creating a positive attitude

It is therefore suitable for both those who have such severe spelling problems they often can manage to write only an approximation of the word they wish to express, and those who make a few spelling errors in most of their paragraphs.

This guide caters for "students" within the age range of seven to seventy or beyond. They may well be able to read, some fluently, and form the letters (although they may confuse them or write 9 for P)! and some of them will indeed be capable of achieving high scores on selected tests of intellectual ability, but most of them in fact have Specific Learning Difficulties, to a greater or lesser degree. The main concern of this book is the teaching of spelling to non-spellers, but the other learning problems which may accompany the spelling difficulty, namely co-ordination, mixed laterality and sequencing problems will be briefly touched on also. We purposely avoid using the term "dyslexia" for important reasons which will be explained in Chapter 2.

Clearly, difficulties in reading and spelling are inseparably linked, so this spelling guide with its structured system will benefit slow readers. Reading is vital for providing the words for spelling, but some bright, fluent readers with good vocabulary and logical reasoning are unable to reproduce accurately in their own writing even simple words which they have just read! We can understand mystified parents being annoyed with them for "laziness", but Chapter 3 of this guide will explain how a type of reading (more like "SEEING") which emphasises the patterns of the letters within the words can be taught to such students, who should then make progress with their spelling, aided by the structured spelling lists in this guide.

This guide does not contain exercises, which may be rather artificial, and we have tried to avoid using as examples obscure words neither school children nor adults need to spell. This guide is meant to be used in a one-to-one situation as a structured learning aid – spelling problems are INDIVIDUAL and INDIVIDUAL help from a parent or spouse provides the most vital assistance. Helpers will also be able to correct their students' errors constructively, by referring to rules, explanations or exceptions: thus, informed correction of one word (instead of merely writing the letters correctly) should teach the students how to spell MANY SIMILAR words in future.

We wrote this book because we found the need for a comprehensive, systematic yet sympathetic guide suitable for helping individual students at home and our advice and methods have largely been derived retrospectively by studying our students' needs and problems. Non-spellers need time and obviously will always have some problems, but we have been heartened by the wonderful progress most of our students have made, and humbled by the effort they have put in. This book does not gloss over the reality of the burden that Specific Learning Difficulties can be, but it does aim to improve performance, rather than merely to explain and accept the status quo. It also aims to pass on the cheerful attitude of our students and our excitement at the possibility of progress – advice is given to parents in Chapter 2 on how to introduce the extra work to reluctant children in the least painful way!

Parents, concerned that in the present economic climate resources will not be available for their children to receive the necessary remedial help with their spelling problem at school, can safely and confidently use this practical guide at home to assist their children's progress. We are acquainted with excellent special needs teachers who bitterly regret their inability to give their pupils sufficient time to overcome their handicap. Pupils who can read are rightly not their first priority, so back up work at home would benefit those children also. Liaison with school is vital: we are partners in our attempts to eradicate the children's problem.

Similarly, wives or husbands can use these methods to help their spouse to cope with the paperwork promotion brings, or cope with the children's homework: writing in a "code" others sometimes cannot decipher properly is a severe handicap in the twentieth century. Accuracy is essential in the work situation.

The book should also be useful for teachers, both those who feel their training on the teaching of spelling was inadequate and those who are puzzled and upset by the low standard of written work which some of their seemingly bright pupils consistently produce.

"All my life I've seen words but I've never really seen them till now. I'm going to start writing my own cheques!" exclaimed Sally, a middle-aged voluntary student. Later chapters will enable readers to help their students to SEE words properly.

Firstly, however, helpers need a full understanding of Specific Learning Difficulties and the problems faced by the many students who have to struggle with them, as progress will only be made when frustration and tension are relieved and positive attitudes established.

CHAPTER 2

HOW SPELLING PROBLEMS CAN REALLY BE "A PAIN IN THE NECK!"

"What is a Clinical Psychologist doing writing a chapter in a book entitled 'Overcoming the Spelling Block'?" you may ask. "Surely Clinical Psychologists work in hospitals or G.P. Health Centres dealing with medical or psychosomatic problems?"

Quite true, we do! and that is exactly how I discovered how widespread were the problems associated with Specific Learning Difficulties.

Although child referrals were only a part of my professional case load it was my work with the Consultant Paediatricians in the District Health Authority that made me aware just how many children suffered from such problems.

A typical referral from a Consultant Paediatrician would be:

"Please see Johnny . . . He has been admitted with recurrent abdominal pain. His parents report that the pain starts regularly on Sunday night and lasts on and off till Friday. The child is doubled up in agony and is frequently sent home from school. The G.P. has tried x,y,z, preparations without success. The parents are sensible people and confirm the child really is in genuine pain. On the ward the pain was present initially, but for the past few days has not re-appeared. Please see and advise."

Now, NOT ALL intermittent abdominal pain is of psychosomatic origin. The child may well have a grumbling appendix or some other physical complaint that can be dealt with by surgery or medication. But if all tests prove negative it could well be that the physiological effects of anxiety and stress are causing PHYSICAL PAIN. Therefore, unless the underlying problems giving rise to anxiety and stress are defined and dealt with, the pain is likely to persist – which is where the Clinical Psychologist comes in.

I would begin by having an informal chat with the parents while the child played with toys in another room. If the parents confirmed that the pain rarely occurred during school holidays and the earlier part of the weekend then we would explore the possibility that it might be something connected with the school environment that was causing stress. The cause needn't be Specific Learning Difficulties: the child could be bullied or dislike school dinners – there could be many reasons.

I would then see the child on his/her OWN. We would have a friendly chat about football, T.V. etc. and then do some standard psychological tests. An analysis of these might reveal the presence of a learning difficulty – spelling, reading or mathematical. On many of the subtests the child might obtain high or very high scores indicating good intellectual ability. Such a discrepancy of scores DOES NOT mean that Johnny or Mary is lazy, dull or mentally handicapped. Specific Learning Difficulties affect people of all levels of intellectual ability – a professor's child with an I.Q. in the top 5% of the general population as easily as the child of a person who never even sat a C.S.E. Indeed, the brighter the child, the more he is liable to feel a failure when repeatedly shown up for poor spelling. But how can I be sure the Specific Learning Difficulties I detected in the child's test results are the cause of the abdominal pain?

My answer is that over 27 years of working in the N.H.S. and seeing hundreds of children with the problems of learning difficulties and physical complaints associated with them, in the majority of cases the presenting problems – be they abdominal pain, migraine, enuresis, encopresis or behavioural – have all tended to LESSEN and have often DISAPPEARED COMPLETELY once the spelling, reading (or both) problems have been resolved.

By the time the child reaches around 8 years of age there is usually an overlay of discouragement on the existing problem of learning difficulties. We know it can be EXASPERATING when, after a period of teaching, the child reproduces the identical error the next day! But the good news is that children with Specific Learning Difficulties are NOT NON-LEARNERS. It takes time, patience, PRAISE and EFFORT but you can win through in the end. This is why I dislike the term "dyslexia": true dyslexia has been defined by an eminent neurologist as "a maturational deficiency of the brain". Very few people have that problem, thousands have Specific Learning Difficulties. Another eminent professor of psychology stated that from his experience as many as 25% of children who encountered difficulties at school were likely to be suffering from Specific Learning Difficulties of one sort or another.

Giving a child a label of "dyslexia" sadly has often resulted in the child's giving up, and all the adults around him writing him off. Herein lies the danger. An ingenious person will go to great lengths to disguise the problem – but the strain of so doing can even cause stress in later life. One adult of 40 years was referred to me by the cardiologists as he had been admitted as an emergency to the coronary care unit on three separate occasions. Each episode had been a false alarm. We eventually found this man had a terrible spelling problem and as he progressed in his job the effort of hiding his difficulties caused so much stress that he was suffering acute chest pain.

Yes, the answer was instruction from an enlightened schoolmaster. That referral was 15 years ago and the man still hasn't had a coronary!

Saying a child has a learning difficulty must NOT become another label. A "difficulty" presents a challenge: "When the going gets tough the tough get going!" someone has said elsewhere. We know from experience learning problems respond to appropriate and adequate help, so the wise Paediatrician or G.P. who rules out a physical abnormality after thorough investigation and refers on to a psychologist only points the child in the right direction to the mastery of the handicap. The diagnosis of Specific Learning Difficulties by a psychologist or other competent specialist using standardised and well validated tests will prove useless if NOTHING MORE is done. Sadly, a few children I have seen have not received the recommended help and have not progressed and, worse still, they have a persistent feeling of inferiority for the future.

Eventual success will depend upon patient teaching, praise and encouragement by parents and teachers for EFFORT and GOOD RESULTS and, most of all, upon the COURAGE of the child who accepts that he will have to spend more time than his classmates and siblings doing extra work through no fault of his own. Parents must realise that accurate spelling requires a very great mental effort for those who have no aptitude for the work. Tiredness will cause work to deteriorate dramatically and it is quite normal to find the same word with three different spellings on the same page! Have hope! Drill and cheerful patience will eventually win the day!

No child can be expected willingly to forego a T.V. programme his brothers and sisters are enjoying for the dubious privilege of learning spellings! This is why I advocate "Behaviour Modification" methods. Some parents at first say, "Oh, that's just bribery!" – but think a minute! How many of you would get out of a warm bed to go to work on a snowy morning if there was no pay packet at the end of the week?

Incentives need not necessarily involve money; staying up later at the weekend or some special treat not normally given is often just as effective.

The important point about this method, which is called "OPERANT CONDITIONING" is that the reward should be immediate (not a bike promised on Feb. 1st but given at Christmas), and seen to be CLEARLY RELATED to the task completed.

Two further points: If the agreed work is not done the reward is withheld. Also siblings must earn their own right to share the reward if it is a family treat.

I suggest a weekly chart or diary is used, with a space for the task to be completed each day. Suggested tasks are
1. to learn and be tested on a structured spelling list from this guide
or 2. to undertake a special dictation as described in Chapter 3
or 3. to do half an hour's general reading suitable to taste, such as football programmes, car manuals, cookery books, music magazines etc.

For each day a tick is recorded in the diary – or a star placed on a wall chart for a younger child – and the incentive (reward) is agreed at the beginning of the week and given, or withheld, at the end of the week. This must be CLEARLY UNDERSTOOD by child and parents. It works!

Personally, I was more interested in the "blanks" than the "ticks" when the parents returned to me with the diary or chart. An analysis of what was happening in the child's life on those days frequently yielded valuable clues to the problem.

Siblings, especially those who can read and spell better than the pupil MUST be kept out of the way. Moreover any comment such as, "Our Johnny is thick!" or gales of mocking or patronising laughter at his mistakes must be severely punished.

For real success the child must improve his visual memory of words all through the day, not just for the short time of an extra lesson. He can be encouraged to find fun in studying the patterns of letters on signs, road names, pubs and shops whilst travelling (adults beware, a driver once nearly had a motor accident doing this!).

Finally a word to teachers and parents: You have NOT DONE ANYTHING WRONG if a child is revealed as having Specific Learning Difficulties but you WILL fail the child if you take no action after the learning problems have been detected.

Students of Piaget who advocate leaving a child to develop and "flower" at his/her own rate are probably right in the majority of cases – but children who suffer from Specific Learning Difficulties require "FERTIL-ISER" in the form of additional tuition. As mentioned in Chapter 1, spelling problems are individual and parents giving individual tuition using this guide are giving invaluable assistance.

What then do we mean by Specific Learning Difficulties? Theories abound. Many specialists have noted a correlation between difficulties in co-ordination and learning difficulties of one sort or another. Others stress the influence of mixed laterality (left/right confusion). A further theory postulates differences in eye scanning as an important factor.

Whatever the basic cause, mixed laterality, co-ordination or visuo-spacial difficulties the child quickly develops an emotional overlay of discouragement, which adds to the problem. Anxiety and stress are NOT "just in the mind" – the physiological effects of anxiety are in the body too. The mind and the body are so linked that anxious thoughts automatically set in motion changes in the body such as increased secretions of adrenalin, heightened muscle tension, rapid breathing patterns etc. This is nature's way of preparing us to meet dangerous situations, giving us extra energy for "fight or flight". These switch off automatically once the danger has passed; but if the "perceived danger" is an essay at school next day or despair over spelling problems, a child cannot run away from the "danger" and unless he/she receives help and encouragement cannot "fight" it. Hence the tense muscles can lead to abdominal pain or headaches, the adrenalin to stomach upsets and the breathing irregularities to palpitations, or even chest pains in adults. The child is not "putting it on" to be excused school, nor the adult to remain off work – they ARE in pain but surgery won't relieve the distress. The only cure is to deal with the source of the anxiety – namely the child's worry about his under-achieving at school, or the adult's concern that his spelling problem will lead to the sack!

My experience has been that with patient tuition, praise and behaviour modification methods, children and adults DO LEARN – slowly maybe at first – but the pace and the enthusiasm increase as progress becomes evident. The joy and happiness that even a little achievement brings is sufficient reward for parent, spouse and teacher.

The good news for the Consultant Paediatrician and the Clinical Psychologist has in so many cases been the report from parents and child, when they return to the Outpatient Clinic after some weeks, that the presenting problems – pain, bed-wetting, episodes of bad behaviour etc. are diminishing, or even have disappeared altogether.

Thankfully not all children who have Specific Learning Difficulties appear to have physiological problems also.

11

I have highlighted these as naturally it was the children who had physical complaints and were sent to a clinical rather than an educational psychologist who were seen by me.

It is vitally important that parents and spouses should try not to transmit their own very understandable worry regarding the spelling and other problems to the "sufferer", as this can only increase the general tension. But you will say, "Don't parents react in the same way to 'perceived danger'? Surely they are in the same situation where 'flight or fight' is impossible?"

This is where we hope our book may help: it is intended to help both parents, spouses, teachers and children fight the stigma of illiteracy, and where action is possible then tension decreases and the autonomic nervous system quietens down.

CHAPTER 3

LEARNING TO SEE WORDS

It would appear from my experience that students with spelling difficulties seem to lack the innate visual memory of the pattern of letters within a word; to help them it is necessary to focus their attention by isolating first the word and then the letters within it. I recommend to helpers the following methods which I use with success: Discover your students' individual spelling problems by dictating a short passage from a book or paper. To put a particular word in focus either buy a set of small magnetic letters (not capitals as these cause confusion), or write your own individual letters on cards. Write out corrected words in small letters, preferably using printing rather than joined writing, and emphasise by colour or underlining the correct version of the letters your students got wrong. Never emphasise by using capital letters in the middle of words, as this may well be an error they make! Relate their errors to the rules detailed in this guide, consolidate the rules and explain exceptions.

A spelling test should be set as a learning aid, not as a trap, so it should consist of certain patterns like "ai" words, words ending "-dge" or "tion" etc. like the structured lists in this Chapter.

Check that your students can recite the alphabet in order, (I know of a bright ten year old junior bookworm who still needed this to be taught to him)! and teach the so called "childish" alphabet, repeating NOT the name (Ay, Bee, See, Dee) but the SOUND of each letter, after a simple word beginning with the sound, thus: apple – "a"; bat – "b"; cat – "c"; dog – "d". It is particularly CONFUSING to say the alphabet names M, N, and R, as students usually have problems in spelling words containing the sounds these letters' names make, so teach the SPELLING of the SOUNDS "em" (empty), "en" (enemy) and "ar" (art), referring to the dictionary for more examples; and, as already suggested, teach the SOUND ONLY of each alphabet letter: mum – "m", nut – "n" and run – "r".

Later you can focus attention on longer words split into syllables to help with sequencing problems, as most students tend to miss out letters. Print a word split thus: in/vi/ta/tion and after study fold over the paper and let the students write the word, then compare theirs, e.g. "invision" – and correct, explaining how many syllables they have missed out.

When you have gained some idea of your students' spelling problems and have studied in the following pages of this guide the solutions to them, you should gradually be able to predict some of their errors and should then be able to give special dictation from a newspaper or magazine, using interesting material according to your students' tastes and abilities, thus: Go through a paragraph first with the students underlining with red biro the part of the words you guess might cause them problems: e.g. emphasise "r", and "-ed" denoting past tense if they tend to miss these out, stress the pattern of the letters in consonant strings and the ending "-ful" (one "l" only). Then dictate in short phrases and constructively correct and discuss errors, relating corrections to the rules in this guide, thus teaching many more spellings in the process.

Parents of secondary school children can help by going through their exercise books for every subject (not just English) and noting down the words they REPEATEDLY spell wrongly – THOSE are the spellings which are most necessary for that individual child. Again, correct errors constructively. Similarly, helpers of adult non-spellers should write down for them the difficult words they NEED to write at work or at home and relate them to the rules. Then the adult can practise spelling the words he/ she really needs and learn other spellings in the process.

(A) SEEING AND HEARING CONSONANTS

Most of my students initially have problems in spelling correctly words which contain consonant blends like the following, whose pattern they find hard to grasp: bl, br; ch, chr, cl, cr; dr; fr; gr; ph, pl, pr; sc, sh, sk, sp, st, scr, shr, spl, spr, str; th, thr, tr; wh, wr; etc. The most common faults are reversing the position of the letters, usually in the middle of words e.g. "slpash" (splash), "forzen" (frozen) – here the following vowel is involved in the confusion, or sliding the position of letters e.g. "sorce" (score) "agasint" (against). Often, as with these examples, all the letters are present in the word although in the wrong order, but sometimes students miss out letters in consonant blends e.g. "pize" (prize), "siek" (shriek).

In order to discover your students' individual problems, dictate words beginning with different consonant blends. For examples refer to a Junior Dictionary – I use the Oxford Junior Dictionary published by Oxford University Press – ISBN 0/19/9102414. Bearing in mind the effort required for your students to force the letters into place, make them see and hear their errors and then look up and say lists of other words beginning with the blends which they found unfamiliar – for this I again use the Junior Dictionary. Write headings in a notebook and encourage your students to group and record these unfamiliar words, leaving space to add more words from books, papers and their own written work. It is harder to think of words with the blends in the middle or at the end like industry, church, progress and grasp – again, the students should list and record examples in the notebook as they occur.

15

Each word should be corrected carefully and con-structively: for example, I ask a schoolboy the terrible word instruction: he pauses, thinks and writes "in tion", the precise pattern of "str" eludes him so he finally slides it in thus: "intrustion", also missing out the "c". I praise him for remembering -tion for "shun" and for being able to sound out what he has in fact written. Then we emphasise the "c" like a precise Scot and we sound out several times "str", each letter separately, then the blend together. Then he studies and reads out to me a page of words beginning with "str" from the Junior Dictionary. We laugh: he has also written "panty" for pantry and for groups a strange sounding new space tribe – "gurops"! It is important to avoid tension – words are fun!

Helpers should also find the following hints on teaching consonants useful: Emphasise r when it appears in a word for it is often left out, I suspect because r is usually the last sound a child learns to pronounce and in words like "govern" you cannot hear it clearly.

In the notebook list the two alternative ways of spelling the sound "juh" at the end of words, leaving space for more examples:

-age	-dge
cabbage	ledge
luggage	wedge
stage	gadget

Soft "c" before "e", "i" and "y" could easily be "s" (cycle to the centre's cinema). Go through the words beginning with soft "c" in the Junior Dictionary, and do the same with soft "g" before "e" and "i" (gentleman's gin). Emphasise "cc" when it occurs in words like accident, success and access.

Teach from the dictionary lists of words with a silent initial or second consonant: (g)narled etc.; (k)nee; (p)salm; (w)rap; w(h)ack and (w)ho.

There are four alternative ways of spelling the sound "shun", sadly, the students' favourite – "shun" is not one of them! Students should copy these lists into their books, leaving spaces for more examples as they occur. I have marked off with/a shorter word which gives a clue as to the correct ending. The ending -sion has a slightly different sound, something like "sjun".

-ssion	-tion
progress/ion	prevent/ion
profess/ion	protect/ion
discuss/ion	detention
session	station
mission	information

-cian	-sion
politic/ian	decision
music/ian	precision
electric/ian	incision
physic/ian	confusion
technic/ian	revision

(B) SEEING AND HEARING VOWELS

1. Perhaps because the sounds are so similar, most of my students fail initially to translate the short "e" and "i" sound with the appropriate letter; they will leave a gap, interchange the two or use "a" or "u". Fortunately repetition and drill are out of fashion so they find chanting quite a novelty. We repeat as often as necessary a word beginning with each short vowel sound followed by the short vowel itself: apple ("a"); egg ("e"); ink ("i"); office ("o"). uncle ("u"). I then say each short vowel and make them write down the letter. Then we observe and say the short vowels within simple words from a book or paper and use the Oxford Junior Dictionary for examples of words beginning with short vowel sounds. Helpers may well find it difficult to teach their students to hear the difference between short vowels and long, but a grasp of this will save many mistakes eventually. Repeat the following, dealing with one vowel at a time – a line above

17

marks the long vowels and long "e" is $\overline{ee}$:

a/ā (lāte); e/ē̄e (fēet); i/ī (sīde); o /ō (bōne);
u/ū (tūbe)

2. Helpers should then teach how "magic e" lengthens the vowel before it thus:

rat/rāte;   kit/kīte;   not/nōte;   tub/tūbe;
can/cāne;   pin/pīne;   hop/hōpe;   fuss/fūse;
When writing these, highlight the vowel and "magic e" with colour.

3. Short vowels will be followed by "ck"; long vowels by "ke" (short "e" is followed by "ck" and "ē̄e" by "k") thus:

sack/sāke;   peck/sē̄ek;   pick/pīke;
lack/lāke;   neck/wē̄ek;   lick/līke;

stock/stōke;   lucky/flūke;
pocket/pōker;   stuck/rebūke;
Trek has no "c" because it is Dutch – see Chapter 5 on derivations.

4. Section 4 is complicated and is intended for use when the students have mastered the basics. The doubling of consonants:

(a) In words of one syllable ending with "-ed" (like lined and trimmed), and many words of two and some of more syllables the pronunciation of the **preceding** vowel usually helps us to decide whether or not the consonant sandwiched between TWO VOWELS will be doubled. In such words with the verbal endings "-ed" and "-ing" the long vowels have 1 following consonant and the short 2 – we chant, "Short vowels have two consonants: a 2, e 2, i 2, o 2, u 2!" This rule has a few exceptions, but it is well worth learning because, in my experience, vagueness about this rule, which involves so many words in every-day use, causes a vast quantity of errors. I have seen errors like "dinning", "begining", "writting" and "stoped" so often I sometimes get confused myself! Use different

18

colours to highlight the consonant (meat) between the vowels (bread).

Examples of words with the verbal endings "-ed" and "-ing":

rāting/happened;	feeling/telling;
scrăped/scrapped;	sleeping/letting;
wrĭting/swimming;	hōping/hopping;
dĭning/beginning;	phōned/stopped;
fūsed/fussed;	
tūbing/running;	

Exceptions include benefited, developed, galloped and focused.

(b) Many two or more syllable words ending "-er" have double consonants after a short vowel before a following vowel such as: battery, letter, seller, fitter, shopper, gutter; similarly, words ending with "y" (I class "y" when it sounds as short or long "i" as a vowel): happy, jelly, witty, floppy, sunny. With the endings "-ing", "ed", "-ence", "-er" words with the accent on the first syllable have 1 r and those on the second 2. e.g. diff'ered 1 r; deferred' 2 r.

1 r: or'dering, or'dered, off'ering, off'ered, diff'erence
2 r: transferred', occurred', referred', inferr'ing

N.B. The change in accent from first syllable to second gives us: ref'erence c.f. referred', def'erence c.f. deferred', trans'ference c.f. transferred' etc.

(c) Many other words have 2 consonants after a short vowel before a following vowel (although there are so many exceptions this could not be called a rule), like attend, assistant, pepper, million, difficult, office, committee, discussion, button, upper. Sadly, there are far too many exceptions to learn, just note these when they occur. Exceptions include panel, material, property and opinion (but the initial "o" in opinion is not quite a rounded "short o" as in "opportunity").

19

Studying derivations helps spelling by establishing patterns and it increases vocabulary and an interest in language – see Chapter 5. Some words BEGINNING with a short vowel have a single following consonant, most of them derive from other languages, mainly Latin or Greek, and seem to keep close to the original spelling, e.g. amount (Latin and Old French), amaze, aloud (c.f. allowed), operation.

Prefixes like "**dis**", "**in**", "**mis**", "**un**" keep close to their origins (mainly Latin) and do NOT double their end consonant before a following vowel, but doubling occurs when they are joined to a word beginning with that SAME consonant, e.g. **dis**appear c.f. **dis**/satisfied.; **in**active c.f. **in**/novation – (Latin "in" "novus" – new); **mis**-alliance c.f. **mis**/shapen. Similarly double consonants occur in many words which derive from Latin and have the prefixes "**il**", "**im**" and "**ir**" (usually meaning not), joined to words beginning with the same consonant as the end one of the prefix, e.g. **il**/legal, **il**/legible; **im**/mobile, **im**/measurable; **ir**/regular, **ir**/relevant; and, less obviously, with the prefixes meaning "in" or "on": **il**/lusion ("il" – on, "lusum" – played); **il**/lumination ("il" – upon, "luminare" – to cast light); **ir**/radiate ("ir" – on, "radiare" – to shine). Now we see why **e**/migrate (Latin "e" – from, "migrare" – to depart, remove) has 1 m and **im**/migrate ("im" – into) has 2!

5. The long ī sound written as "-igh" and "-ight" I teach thus: A right handsome knight with fine thighs gave us a fright, so we took flight, as he rode through the night to fight with all his might in sight of the high moon's bright light!

6. The following structured lists of vowel combinations need to be copied out and learnt; again, advise students to leave plenty of space for examples from their own work and encourage them to think of more examples and spot them in books and papers. Deal with each section slowly and separately – remember your students

20

may find what seems obvious to you very difficult to grasp.

ai has a "long a" sound, as does -ay at the end of words:

ai	ay
train	May
sail	today
paint	player

au and aw sound like "or" and there are a few often used words with the spelling aught:

au	aw	aught
automatic	crawl	daughter
laundry	drawn	caught
caution	law	taught

ea sounds as "short e" or "long e" and ee sounds as "long e":

ea	ea	ee
steady	meat	feet
head	speak	geese
bread	dream	street

ie – Students need to put ie rules into practice many times, for the whole scene is sadly like a minefield for them! Teach and consolidate each rule separately: 1. "i" before "e" except after "c", most of these words rhyme with "ee". 2. If it is after "c" it's "e" before "i". 3. The exceptions don't usually rhyme with "ee" apart from "seize" etc. and I happen to say "either" with a "long i"! 4. Names, as usual, don't follow the rules:

ie	cei
thief	receipt
chief	ceiling
field	conceited
piece	deceive
believe	conceive
niece	perceive
friend	receive

21

ei	**names**
neighbours	Neil
height	Keith
weight	Sheila
reign	
leisure	
eight	
vein	

oa sounds as "long o" and ow sometimes sounds as "long o":

oa	**ow**
boat	snow
road	shown
goal	grown

oi causes difficulties but it simply sounds "oy!" – as if someone wants one's attention, as does -oy at the end of words:

oi	**oy**
oil	boy
point	destroy
voice	employ(er)

oo usually sounds like "ooh!" but there are exceptions:

oo	**oo**
balloon	wood
spoon	book
school	good

ou usually sounds as though you've been pinched – "ow!", sometimes it sounds "ooh!" and some words have both the spelling and the sound "ow!" There are well used exceptions ending -ough and -ould.

ou	**ou**	**ow**
cloud	you	cow
shout	group	down
pound	soup	clown

ough	ould
enough	could
thought	should
through	would

ui usually sounds like "ooh!" but in some vowel combinations the "u" is not pronounced:

ui	ua, ui
fruit	guard
juice	guide
suit	build

Group the following vowel combinations with "r" carefully, according to sound:

air	are	ear
chair	care	near
stair	scared	fear
fair	share	dear

ear	ear	eer
wear	early	mountaineer
bear	earth	peer
pear	search	cheer

ir	ire	or
first	fire	born
shirt	wired	sort
girl	hire	port

oar	oor	ore
oar	poor	more
board	floor	stores
roar	door	score

our	our	ur
our	four	turn
sour	pour	burnt
flour	your	fur

The indeterminate ending sound "uh" causes problems; the most usual spellings are -"er" or -"or" but there are four other alternative spellings:

-er	-or (jobs)
sister	conductor
manager	doctor
river	inspector
computer	instructor
producer	author
order	contractor
employer	professor

-or (others)	-ar
error	sugar
motor	radar
mirror	regular
resistor	circular
transistor	nectar
terror	particular
reactor	grammar

-our	-re	-ure
colour	metre	measure
humour	centre	leisure
favour	acres	figure
armour	sombre	feature
savoury	spectre	creature

The ending which sounds like "-ul" is often "-le" but there are two alternative spellings to be learnt:

"-le": Settle a little nettle in a kettle but mind the handle in the middle!

"-al": Electrical, mechanical and technical staff at the local hospital were given medals made of musical metal petals.

"-el": A model train with a flannel funnel swivels as it travels through the Channel tunnel with labels on its panels and a camel in a large barrel.

24

"-ed": Many of my students miss off this past tense ending when writing, but not when speaking. Sadly, some schools teach little grammar now, but I feel a real mastery of the written word demands at least the ability to recognise a verb. Briefly explain this as a "being or doing word, which someone or something is or does." The root (infinitive) is "to . . ." and from this we form the tenses, which tell when the verb went on: e.g. the past tense of "to jump" is "jumped". The past (this morning, yesterday, last year etc.) tense may end in "t", but it often ends -ed: e.g. seemed, scrambled, danced and shouted.

"-y": This is used with a "short i" or a "long i" sound at the end of words (some non-spellers think it should be an "e"!) e.g. I like the lovely company of a baby. I fly through the sky with a loud cry.

CHAPTER 4

HANDY HINTS

1. Adding "s" to a "-y" ending word: the "y" remains if there is a vowel before it but changes to "-ie" if there is a consonant before it:

vowel -y	**vowel -ys**
chimney	chimneys
donkey	donkeys
employ	employs

cons. -y	**cons. -ies**
fly	flies
berry	berries
cry	cries

The "y" is retained before the ending "-ing" but changes to "ie" before the ending "-d":

-ying	**-ied**
trying	tried
spying	spied
frying	fried

2. Remove "e" before adding "-ing": write / writing; hope / hoping; slope / sloping.

3. Remove one "l" from "full" before adding it to a word: careful; hopeful; joyful and note "skilful". "Fully" has "ll": carefully; hopefully; skilfully.

4. Except for "Lesley" and "-lley" words like alley, valley and trolley etc. words rarely end "-ley" – a very common error. Be aware that "e" ending adjectives become adverbs by adding "-ly": immediate – immediate/ly.

5. I have never had the visual memory of the endings "-ance" or "-ence", "-ant" or "-ent" and "-able" or "-ible". Check with the dictionary when needed and list in the following groups:

-ance	-ant
performance	pleasant
assistance	restaurant
importance	important

-ence	-ent
reference	agreement
presence	equipment
difference	different

Note "y" changes to "i" in words like appliance and reliance. To my surprise Chambers Dictionary gives both "e" and "a" for dependent, but I think "e" is more usual.

-able	-ible
capable	responsible
breakable	terrible
irritable	edible

Note "e" drops out in lovable. Chambers gives it as optional in rat(e)able but it is retained to soften the "g" in words like changeable and manageable.

6. Apostrophes: I am tempted to advise students (and people who write greengrocery signs) not to use these, as they tend to pepper them around every time they see a word ending in "s"!

(a) The French use a word for "of" but the English give the owner an apostrophe before the "s" if singular, and after if plural, except for men's, women's and children's, which retain an Old English "e" plural. The owner might not be a person, like "day's" in The Beatles' song "A Hard Day's Night".

The pronouns hers, ours, yours, theirs and the adjective its are possessive already and do not require an apostrophe; therefore, :it's" = "it is" and "they're" = "they are".

(b) Students with sequencing problems need to be made aware exactly which letter is missing, otherwise they will put the apostrophe in the wrong place in words like haven't, can't, shouldn't and we're.

7. Students should study the following well used words which are so often incorrectly spelt; the letters which they find strange should be highlighted by colour, which I find very effective:

address	beautiful
business	character
desperate	does
except	first
(un)necessary	neither
receipt	science
special	success
because	beginning
control	definite
eight	empty
idea	know
particular	probably
sincerely	soldier
surprise	usual

8. Pairs and trios: Students' poor visual memory will cause them to confuse pairs and trios of words which sound the same or similar, yet have quite different meanings. Sadly there are scores of these, like bare/ bear; fair/ fare; groan/ grown; principal/ principle etc. It is best not to teach exhaustive lists of these as they might then confuse words they had right in the first place! Simply write down the pairs they get wrong in their written work, using pictures or any personal memory aids you can think of. Do not use exercises as traps – your students have enough problems!

28

It is best to concentrate on the look of one word then the other will be right too. As mentioned before, a little grammar helps, especially the ability to spot a verb. The following is a list of my students' favourites, in which I indicate my own memory aids. Brackets are used (again, readers can use colour) to highlight linked letters and dashes mark off explanations:

(a)ccept – receive – sounds   (e)xcept
   (a) not (e)

angels – heavenly   angles – maths.
b(ea)ch – s(ea)   b(ee)ch – tr(ee)
c(a)ught – c(a)tch   court – yard
h(ear) – (ear)   (he)re – t(he)re
I (know) (no)   way of teaching this
                                       (now)!

A dog licen(c)e – noun as   licen(s)es – verb as
   advi(c)e -   advi(s)e – your dog.
You will l(o)se   that l(oo)se button.
m(ea)t – (ea)t   meet – someone
meter – gas   1,000 metres
minuet – a dance   minute – 60 seconds
A pound (of) butter   fell (off) the shelf.
He pas(sed) – verb -   past the window.
At hockey practi(c)e –   we practi(s)e – verb –
   noun –   hard.
s(hor)e – sea (hor)se   sure – certain
star(e) – (e)ye   stair – case
t(here) – and (here)   their – of them
He thre(w) – from verb   the ball through the
   thro(w) –   window.
(Two) visitors (too) many   came (to) see me.
(Wh)ere are the clothes you   (were) (wear)ing?
(Wh)ich weird wi(t)ch   had a sandwich?
Think of "wh" in (wh)at? (wh)ere? (wh)en? (wh)ich?
   (wh)ose? and (wh)y?

CHAPTER 5

DERIVATIONS AND DICTIONARIES

Words which do not follow the rules often derive from other languages or retain an Old English spelling; pointing this out helps students to remember the words' patterns and assists in fostering an interest in and love of words. Many terms denoting scientific inventions and terms used in other branches of learning are borrowed from Greek or Latin, and one word, like "tele" (Greek – at a distance) "vision" (connected with the Latin for "seen") might combine borrowings from both. Greek influence confuses us with "ph" for "f" in words like pharmacy, telephone, physics and photograph and "ch" pronounced with a hard "k" sound in chemist, character, psychology, technology etc. Greek influence is seen in the use of "y" instead of "i" within words like cycle, system and gymnasium, and terms used in science like hydrogen and polystyrene, and maths terms like symmetry, cylinder and polygon.

Happily, many Latin based words follow the rules, but the Latin influence confuses us in words like emergency, science, scissors, patients and know (Latin – "cognosco", Old English – "cnawan"), where we keep close to the original spelling and anglicise the pronunciation.

Many two or more syllable words ending "-ic" (not "-ick") are borrowed from Latin or Greek: fabric (Latin), electric (both have a similar word), mechanic, politic and microscopic (Greek), to name but a few.

"Oddities" derived from other languages include yacht (Dutch), verandah (Hindi), ski (Norwegian), anorak (Eskimo), and centre, beauty, lieutenant and surprise (French).

Check before you buy an adult dictionary that it contains derivations as these help both spelling and vocabulary work. It is vital that students should be encouraged to risk using a variety of words even though they cannot spell them. Their work would be very dull if they only used words of which they were sure!

The Oxford Junior Dictionary mentioned in Chapter 3 is also excellent for the students' general use, whatever their age. The words are printed in distinctive red and the alphabet, with the letter the page deals with emphasised in red, is printed at the top of each page. The meanings are clearly set out and it also lists at the back the numbers as words (so vital for the writing of cheques), countries, continents, colours, days and months.

Non-spellers who have difficulties with even a junior dictionary because they are not sure where to start when looking up a word, might benefit from also using The A.C.E. Spelling Dictionary by Moseley and Nicol, published by Learning Development Aids – ISBN 0/905 114/16/7, which teaches students to pick out the first strong vowel sound, then the first letter; the index guides users to the correct page where words are grouped in columns according to the number of syllables. This emphasis on the number of syllables is very useful for students who have sequencing problems. The Spelling Dictionary contains few meanings – these are only provided to differentiate between pairs or trios of words which sound the same, like "to", "too" and "two"; as its title suggests the dictionary has been compiled for those who need to check the spelling of words and students who use it will learn more about the actual process of looking up words in a dictionary – this will be good practice for using an ordinary dictionary later on. The

A.C.E. Spelling Dictionary is cheerfully and attractively presented and encourages students to try new words; it may be initially hard to master and most students will probably need patient guidance for a while but they should eventually enjoy using it on their own.

CHAPTER 6

ASSOCIATED LEARNING DIFFICULTIES

As mentioned in Chapter 2 it is often noticed that children with spelling and reading problems are "mixed lateral" – commonly called "ambidextrous". It is considered "clever" to be able to use both hands and a footballer who is equally skilled with both feet is considered an asset to the team. But in the early years of life mixed laterality often means that the child tends to reverse some of his/her letters and this leads to confusion and slowness compared with age peers who do not have the problem. However, frequently when the child reaches teenage years the left/right confusions seem to decrease, but rarely disappear completely.

Imagine the difficulty in mathematics if, in attempting a division, you started from the right rather than the left! But, once more, the good news is that patient teaching, PRAISE and encouragement gain results.

There are many helpful yet simple techniques to assist children who encounter confusions when learning to spell a word correctly. For example it is often recommended that the confusion between b and d can be overcome by suggesting the child writes the word "bed" on a little card, or even on his hand. Then he can be sure he has got the initial letter of "door", "boot", "boat", "date" etc. correct by listening to the relevant sound as he says the word. Similarly, confusion between 9 and p can be avoided by comparing the word with "9 pegs".

Once started on these simple strategies the child will often think up similar ones unaided.

It can be tiresome or even dangerous for children to confuse left and right – we have known one child wait for the bus on the wrong side of the road, one ride down the wrong side of the road and another put out his right hand and turn left! Again, patient repetition and ploys like reminding the child which hand he writes with help; cycling proficiency as taught in many primary schools is also a boon.

Difficulties with sequencing cause children problems in everyday life – some literally do not know what day it is! Children who cannot learn their tables during the regular course of the lesson will GRADUALLY master them by repeated chanting; likewise the alphabet, how many days in each month and the sequence of the days of the week and the months of the year. Some children and adults have intense difficulty in interpreting, for example, "2.11.1990" as the second of November. The months' order can be learnt by using "celebrations" like bonfire night, Christmas, Easter, mum's birthday etc. Parents should keep on the wall a calendar with the poem "Thirty days hath September . . ." pinned to it – this might prevent children writing things like "January 32nd"! Similarly, children may need a lot of practice in telling the time from the clock face – using a cardboard clock and pointing out typical events for each hour may help here. Happily, most children find digital watches much easier to manage.

Sequencing problems can also cause untidiness in subjects like maths and science as the children may be unable to arrange columns etc. evenly across the page: we suggest they measure carefully with a ruler where to start each column until practice makes this unnecessary.

Some children may have co-ordination problems even though they possess great enthusiasm for sport. We would recommend amateur sports clubs, providing they have a policy of accepting children of all levels of ability. Again, if the children are tenacious, coaches who patiently explain, DEMONSTRATE and drill over a length of time may EVENTUALLY achieve results rewarding for themselves and the children, whose confidence will be boosted. We have been impressed by the work of coaches at a local swimming club, where, after two years' patient tuition and drill, we have seen a sturdy twelve year old, not "a natural swimmer" with regards to co-ordination, joyfully master the intricacies of free-style, diving and tumble turns.

CHAPTER 7

ACCURACY MATTERS!

There have been numerous changes in the philosophy of education in the twentieth century – some have been based on careful research – others have been less well substantiated. Since the aim of education is the eventual benefit of the student we wish that those who organise teacher training would proceed with caution and avoid extreme swings in the philosophy of education. We know that in the past drill, including excessive amounts of parsing and analysing, was stifling; but we believe in the need for balance. Leaving aside the demands of examinations, our experience suggests that both creativity and drill are needed to fit pupils for life and for work. We would like to see the whole primary school class spending a little more time each week on structured spelling, rather than risk turning out one or two people who might one day sit like June, aged 35, with hands trembling as she tries to master the mystery of the blend "str". Our educational philosophy would be based on Coleridge's definition of the ideal poet, who combined "a more than usual state of emotion with a more than usual state of order".

We want the students to accept that their mistakes should be corrected, yet we do not want them to be depressed by the resultant litter of red marks! We feel teachers should encourage students by awarding marks for effort and by praising the content of written work. It should be made clear that spelling matters, but it is understood that the students are not lazy or careless. If the student is required to produce a piece of written work in the classroom situation within strict time limits

36

we advise that marking should take into account the child's spelling problem. Nevertheless, when time is not a factor – i.e. homework, accuracy of spelling must be required.

Accuracy matters: if a child using the computer chains in, for example, "Arkdins" instead of "Arcadians" he/she will soon see that the computer will not load the game! Filing clerks know, to their secret shame, that it is in fact because they do not know their alphabet in sequence accurately that the records are in a muddle, and the operators who mangle surnames know the boss can't "find people in the computer" because he/she is keying in a name correctly spelt which is not in there in that form! – we know, because these desperate people confide in us.

As a voluntary student once said, "The simplest note for the boss causes me problems!"

The words he needed were in fact full of problems for a poor speller but, with individual help, he eventually mastered them. He was blessed with a supportive wife and a cheerful attitude.

A word processor "spell check" can be a valuable aid in the work situation as it can quickly detect and correct the majority of spelling errors, although it will not detect errors caused by confusion between pairs of words, and it will not always be able to detect the correct word from a very poor approximation. We are a little concerned that some people use the existence of spell check as an excuse for saying the TEACHING of correct spelling is not as important as it used to be. We would reply that many people do not possess a word processor or spell check and those who do may not be near them when a note or cheque needs to be written or a form filled up and, most importantly, everyone needs the self fulfilment of being able to communicate clearly in written form without the need of extensive correction.

Accuracy is required for loading and saving a file in the computer; the computer itself can be a valuable weapon in the fight for accurate spelling: happily, many secondary school pupils are now taught keyboarding skills and are familiar with both the typewriter and the word processor. Some parents have remarked and we have also observed that such pupils usually seem to make fewer spelling mistakes when typing. We have not researched this matter, but from our limited experience we would suggest that perhaps seeing the letters printed on the keyboard, or memorising them for touch typing, makes these pupils more "letter conscious" which is good for progress. We recommend if parents of such pupils do have a word processor that they encourage them to use it, either for dictation or for short articles of their own creation, and we suggest that, taught by their parents, the pupils correct their own mistakes on screen, using the delete and cursor keys. The students will learn more readily by doing the corrections themselves, it will make a change from the usual litter of red marks and they can have real pride in the final printed version! (As before, helpers should correct constructively afterwards by relating to the rules or exceptions). Although a computer can be useful in these ways it is not essential for progress; paper and pencil and the methods outlined in this guide, backed up by plenty of praise and encouragement will be sufficient to obtain results.

ALL our students know that spelling matters; those people who say it does not can themselves all spell perfectly well. They understand neither the frustrations of bright children who are full of ideas they cannot adequately write down, nor the anxieties of a newly promoted adult facing paperwork for the first time since leaving school, nor the anguish of a mother whose young children can write more words than she can.

We have found our students' tenacity an inspiration – they have shown that Specific Learning Difficulties can eventually be overcome, but first the problem has to be identified and then faced with cheerfulness, patience and effort.

Students suffering from Specific Learning Difficulties are NOT NON-LEARNERS – with the correct approach they achieve IN TIME. Some have even gone on to top careers, and all those who have persevered with their spelling problems have achieved a measure of success they would never have dreamed possible in the early dark days of discouragement and despair, and most importantly, they have led happy and fulfilled lives without the cloud of failure hanging over them.